Dil-Se

Whispers from the Heart

By

Pally Dhillon

Other books by Pally Dhillon

Kijabe (2001)	Amazon.com
Walk with Pride (2008)	Amazon.com
Surkh Haneri (2009)	Lahore Bookshop
Surkh Haneri (2011)	Amazon.com

Foreword

My other two manuscripts, Kijabe and Walk with Pride, included a number of romantic letters which were exchanged by the main characters; and I was encouraged and inspired by readers to compile a collection of these letters into a publication. That was the beginning of this short synopsis of heart felt emotions.

Dil Se, Whispers from the heart, is dedicated to everyone who has experienced the emotions and feelings that are only felt by one in love. These words can only partially express the heartaches, longing and desires that are felt in connection with love. Hopefully, I have done justice to these special feelings. I think it makes for cozy bedside reading

Pally Dhillon

Advance praise for Dil Se, Whispers from the heart

Pally Dhillon's latest literary contribution, Dil Se Whispers from the Heart, is a must read for anyone who has ever been in love or been loved. This collection of love poems and passages touches one's heart like never before. Reading Whispers from the Heart commands the reader to react emotionally to the joy, and sadly, the despair that love can bring. This book would make a beautiful gift on any occasion for that special someone who touches your heart

Winifred L. Zanotti

Very tender, sensitive, loving, caring, and from the heart. Romanticism is not dead. You have proved it to me

Harlan Carey

Pally Dhillon has crafted something special in Whispers From The Heart. The emotional, warm, and intensely powerful love-letters woven together throughout the book provide keen insights to the human nature of love.... beautifully done!

-Ann Z. Bush, M. Ed.

Recommended reading for the romantics at heart. Pally defines the emotions of loveliness and loneliness expressively. The chosen words illuminate his heart's excitement and pain -- all with expressive detail. As a reader, you can experience the roller coaster of ecstasy and agony, which love entails.

Surinder Calay

I am amazed at the diversity with which Pally writes, from historic ancestry in Kijabe to adventures in Walk With Pride. Now comes a different perspective with romance. Even for those "unromantic" souls, there is something in Dil Se, Whispers from the heart that one can relate to, be it a short abstract or poem. Grab a coffee or a glass of wine and enjoy!

Poonam Majhu

Dil Se, Whispers from the Heart is a gentle reminder of the importance of love in one's life and how important it is to share these special feelings one has for another.

To quote the author "love is a rare gift from the gods of love", loving and letting one know they are loved is one of life's best presents. Love is a mystery in many ways.

Dil Se, Whispers from the heart, a good loving read, a good loving present.

Nancy Score

Pally Dhillon, a retired computer professional who lives in Ohio and spends a large amount of the year traveling, is also an author and has written historical fictional books that are set in East Africa. His first book "Kijabe - An African Saga" was published in 2001. Kijabe is the author's recollection of how his grandfather and other Sikh pioneers immigrated from India and settled in East Africa, and Kenya in particular. The novel's main character, Mehar Singh, settled in the small town of Kijabe, and the story surrounds Singh's hard work, determination and adventures. The book also features the experiences of entrepreneurial Sikh immigrants in a foreign and hostile land in the early twentieth century. Dhillon's second book was the Kijabe manuscript translated to the Punjabi dialect and published in 2005 by Lahore Bookshop in India titled Surkh Haneri (Red Wind) and later by Amazon in 2011.

Pally's third book Walk with Pride, published in 2008, is the engrossing story of three Indian patriarchs—Mehar Singh, Shahbaz Khan and Nanak Chand— childhood friends who immigrated to different countries in East Africa in the early 20th Century. The gentlemen's lives are forever intertwined—and changed—through the vagaries of life. Walk with Pride is a well researched historical novel encompassing three generations and the unfolding of their lives in India, Iran, Canada, Tanzania, Uganda and Kenya. The Sikh religion is depicted in terms of the historical sacrifices made by the Sikh Gurus. The theme of this publication is genocide and the storyline takes the main characters from the Indian subcontinent to Iran, Afghanistan, Rwanda and East Africa as they live through and experience the atrocities.

The latest manuscript, Dil Se Whispers From the Heart, is a collection of romantic letters that express deepest emotions and feelings.

Dhillon's interests include reading, sports and technological innovations and trends. Involved in field hockey all his life, he has been active in USA field hockey on the west coast and served as the president of the hockey association, a player, coach and organizer. He has traveled all over the world to play hockey and to watch the Olympics, World Cups and other sporting events. He organized the medal ceremonies and announcements for hockey at the 1976 Montreal games and the 1984 Olympics in Los Angeles.

His new sporting passion is Golf and he loves enjoying his family and his three exciting grandchildren, Isabella, Leo and Maya.

1

My love, my heart,

I missed you more today than yesterday. Now it hurts because we don't talk enough and the mind wanders back to what we had...or in simple language, plain memories. This is the first time that I realized how many of these memories there are. I think we have collected enough in such a short time...what some people might experience in a lifetime and sadly, some will never have any. We all make choices in life and then we have to live with them right or wrong. I know I made the right one.

On Tuesday I missed your second call. A sharp pain went through my heart. In the back of my mind I know this is silly, but I felt this might have been our last call and I missed it. I love you so much. I think of all the silly things you do and say...and little things you remember, like the song I like. And you say my name so softly. I love the way you say my name. It never sounded as lovable or pretty or romantic before. It was just a name, and you made it special and gave it feelings.

I just finished reading "The Notebook." I read it in two evenings. It was amazing how I could relate to nearly every page in the book. There is one thing I want you to do for us. I want you to write about all of our moments together, so if anything happens to one of us, the other will have this to hold on to.

I want to die with them in your arms, and you kissing me and me kissing you. Maybe if we leave this place together, then god will have to keep us together. I don't trust you getting up there before me, because you don't have the patience to wait for me.

When we are together holding each other, I always listen to our heartbeats to see if they beat together in unison. Somehow I believe that my heart makes yours beat. I always get this thought that this will be one of our miracles... that if ever one of us ends up in the hospital, we will shock the medical world by making one's heart beat with the other's, with no machines attached. I know this is true, we live because of each other. You are not complete without me, and I need you to make me complete.

My love, just think of all the things that we have done. You taught me to golf and I taught you to cook. We taught each other the importance of just having one good friend instead of all the ones with whom we hung around. I taught you how to bike, but we still need to do more. You have taught me how to feel good about myself.

I have learned to ignore a lot of things about people...and about spending my precious time trying to fit into a society that does nothing for anyone but feed their own egos. Today, I wouldn't care if no one spoke to me. I just want to be with you and spend my lifetime with you.

We can write about skiing, golf, the beach in Rio, and the day you thought we were going to drown. I am glad we didn't. Think of all the times that we have been together since. We would never have experienced all those happy moments. All the times your plane was late and I picked you up at odd times, and how we made love in interesting places.

I also want you to remember our first dinner together. I know you did love me a little then, though you don't want to admit it. I think you loved me more than you think. I did want you to kiss me that night. I wish you had. That was the reason I didn't respond to you because I was afraid of what I wanted. I wish we had danced that night...and every night.

I wait for your phone calls every morning and sleep with the phone

 next to me, just in case.

Love me always.

2

I've been anxiously waiting to see the sun rise, take a stroll on the soft white sandy beach at Captiva, and feel the cool breeze floating across the gulf brushing my cheeks. I follow the Manatees as they mate right next to the shore. I have been waiting to feel your touch, waiting for our love to blossom, waiting for my journey to begin, waiting for a union that would never end.

Now I have all of these rare things and so much more. My dream came true the day I met you. I have traveled a long, difficult, and tiresome road looking for you. The thorns along the way left deep cuts in my ego and outlook. I looked for true love but found nothing except heart-aches. Then finally, there you were, my love.

When your eyes met mine, I swore that you could see into my soul, and all of my past injuries healed. Finally, I felt alive. Now when I travel that road, the world looks real. I see roses blooming in place of the thorns because of my love for you. It has been so difficult for me to tell you this, but I love you. It's amazing how much those three little words can mean. Yet they're not nearly enough to describe my heartbeats that are synchronized with yours and only yours. When I think of the life that we'll spend together, I'm filled with longing joy and excitement. I only want to make love to you and I want to show you how much I care about you. If only there were stronger words to express what I feel for you...but for now, "I love you" will have to do. But imagine how wonderful it is going to be when I am with you, my love.

3

My heart, my Shan,

Each night before I sleep, I wait for your voice on the phone. Your sweet voice echoes through my mind. As I rest my head on my pillow, a smile seeps through my soul, knowing that you and you alone have made me whole. Without you I would simply be surviving, but with you I am living life to the fullest. Because of your love, my spirit has been rejuvenated. The simplest pleasures in life bring me so much joy that when I think of you and me, it is hard to find the words to describe them. Even in our bad, angry moods, regardless of the irritations of daily life, we manage to make each other laugh. The sound of your laughter rings through my ears and touches my heart. Your captivating smile triggers tingling warmth inside me. The difference between you and me are very few, yet they are there. However, we accept those differences, embracing them because they are part of something we love about one another.

It isn't about looks nor money, but the simplic-
ity in life that we find so attractive...know-
ing we could survive anywhere as long as we
are together. Love is not a job, love simply is.
Unconditional love is what I offer you, and from
you I receive the same. You are my heart of
hearts, my soul mate, friend, lover, and part-
ner for life.

I will love you forever and a day. Thank you for
being there, loving me and knowing what my
true heart wants.

I love you so much and will miss you even more
while you are gone. Have a great trip.

Your Ashna

4

My love,

When I think of you, I think of a red rose that is beautiful and is the embodiment of something pure, something to touch with care, something so precious that one just wants to hold it forever in a safe place.

You are my rose that I would like to have...and carry with me everywhere. I would touch it, smell it, and caress it every now and then. I am so lucky that you are all mine and that I love you so much, my precious.

Nobody loves you like I do.

I still remember how I felt the first time you touched me. In that single moment I became yours forever. And with every touch since then I want to be with you forever and forever.

What I'm really trying to say when I say "I love you"... I am trying to work a miracle—that of actually being able to say all the million and one things I'm feeling deep inside my heart. To try and tell you how much I love you is to attempt the impossible, relying on words and sentences that fall so far short of the exquisite feelings that live in my heart and the impossible happiness that is always on my mind.

When I say "I love you," I find myself hoping that somehow you know how deeply and wonderfully that feeling goes.

When I need more than words to tell you these feelings, it is my prayer that you can see the love...in my eyes, in my smiles, even in the gentle fold of my hands...within your hands. And I hope you'll always understand, whether the perfect words are spoken or not, that when I say "I love you" and I hug you, I'm really trying to say that.

There isn't a dream that could ever come true and would make me happier than all this.

I love you so much.

5

Anar, my soul,

I miss you so much and I feel for you under these conditions. If we were together, I would hold you close to my heart, let our heartbeats talk to each other, hug you forever, and never let you go.

I'm going to write to you and try to put into words these feelings that I have for you. Please forgive me, my darling, for my amateurish writing and clumsy thoughts. You know that you are the writer in this union. I am only the legal mind, and I regret that I cannot produce the elegant and eloquent phrases which would do justice to my feelings for you.

How can I capture on this page what I feel? These are such strong emotions that words can't even begin to touch the depth of what I feel. This phenomenon may be expressed simply by the word "love," or at least it may be the closest word in the English language. So let me say that "I love you" from dawn to sunset, from moment to moment, in between the breaths I take, and any time that is left over.

The dream goes on...and my wish is for this joyful, serene, blissful and happy "sleep" to go on infinitely. My love for you strengthens and deepens by the day, and now that I know you so well I feel you to be an extension of myself. When you hurt, I hurt. When you cry, I cry. When you feel joy, your joy and laughter thrills me. When I do not see the beauty of your face or hear your magical voice, I feel that I am only half alive. Without you, I am only half of what I could be.

You bring out the best in me. You make me feel as I have never felt before. You listen to me and often anticipate my next thought or sentence, and I do the same for you. Our interests are so alike that it is scary at times, even though our personalities are different. I agree with you so frequently that it could be perceived that I was doing it deliberately, but the crazy thing is that I'm not. We simply agree on a variety of things.

The heartaches, the skipping of heartbeats, the everlasting desire to be with you all the time are feelings that teenagers are supposed to experi- ence. I would never have dreamt that I could experience this.

We long to touch and caress each other, and our lips have to be forced apart. I can't explain this, and I wish I could. When I am with you, there seems to be no track of time and it passes so quickly that it is not fair as our time together is limited.

I love the way you hold and hug me. Could there be a better fit? I love the way you close your eyes when I hold you, how you keep your eyes closed when I am kissing you, when you rest your head on my shoulder. I love the way you touch me when we walk or sit or chat. I love the way you hold my arm when we walk. I love the way you sneak up on me and hug from the back.

At times I think of pinching myself to find out if this is a dream or reality that I am experiencing. I could go on and on, I do love you and will forever.

I find it amazing how this trickle of emotions has blossomed into an ocean of everlasting love that is so strong, yet is unconditional with no demands. I long to be near you, yet even when I am far away and I can hear your voice it seems that you are within me and beside me.

I can look into your beautiful hazel eyes that intrigue me to such an extent that I can gaze at them forever. I wish that everyone could experience the happiness that I do when we are together or when I think of the times that we have spent with each other.

True love is rare to find, and I am so lucky to have found it. So now you know how treasured you are to me. I do hope that you feel the same. It is exceptional to come across someone so special whom you can love and trust and feel completely at ease with as though they were part of your own essence, body and mind. I have all that with you.

When I lie down or when I am sitting, I close my eyes and think of your caressing fingers running over my arms and body, and your soft, tender, moist, inviting lips touching mine in the distinctive way that only you can kiss. As we kiss longer, our lips become more passionate and they move sensuously with our tongues becoming inflamed. As our hips move closer and closer with our chests close, our heartbeats seem to synchronize so that it could be one heart beating. As our fingers and hands take over, our body temperatures soar.

When the concept emerges that I will not be able to see you, I feel very sad. I do know that whatever is meant to be, will be. And I believe I now know what a writer meant when he wrote, "Absence makes the heart grow fonder."

My love, I can't live without you and I can't exist without you. You truly must come back here as soon as you can. Every fraction of a second that I am away from you, it seems like being in a vacuum. I feel as though I am adrift on a sea without my life vest, and my mind is always with you rather than being centered on the work I need to be doing. Please also know that when you ache, I ache. When you mourn, I feel the pain. I am your alter ego, and I am experiencing everything you are going through. But the pain you are in now must end and we must return to our normality. As long as you are in agony and feeling depressed, you imprison me there as well. I beseech you to set me free as you free yourself from this tortured state.

I love you so much and will never stop as long as there is air to breathe. I love you and wish you were here right now. Come back soon, my love.

Yours Akash

Anar had been reading the letter at her ailing father's bedside. She began sobbing as she read the last lines. Her mother asked what was wrong, but she was embarrassed and explained that it was a note from a dear friend who missed her and was trying to encourage her.

6

My dearest Akash,

I miss you and I love you more than ever, more than words can express. Now that I am a journalist, let me write a reporting on my feelings for you. Perhaps I can be a little philosophical.

There are moments in life when one wishes that time would stand still, that everything would stay the way it is, forever. Such happy times could be periods of emotional or physical joy, mental stimulation, or times when we feel a oneness with the world, or with someone close to our heart. The thoughts and feelings one experiences are so unique, joyful, soothing and pleasant. We feel as though we are on top of the world and want to stay there.

Such a moment could be a time of great achievement in academics, sports, business or career, but more often those moments of transcendence come with the birth of a child, the closeness of family, or the first kiss of a new love.

Memories of wonderful times can be triggered by listening to a piece of music, the lyrics of a song, or words heard during a conversation. Though these moments are private, we get the urge to tell everyone and share that overwhelming inner happiness.

But when love is the source of these feelings, those moments are carved much deeper in the mind. Feelings of transcendence, the desire to share this feeling with everyone around you, that connectedness to the one you love...these feelings are stronger, and the degree of emotional satisfaction or physical happiness is at a higher level. In a situation where two individuals are in love, there are bound to be moments of joy and fulfillment. There are times when we wish we had a crystal ball and could gaze into the future, so we could see the friendships that might develop or know how long they might last.

From afar, I recognize and distinguish a change in you, although I'm sure you don't perceive that. This could stem from the fact that I am getting to know you as only a soul mate knows it's true other self.

I confide in you, which I have never done with another being. This trust is based on knowing that you and I respect our unique bond and relish our intimacies.

I wish you could open up to the level that I do, and this might happen with time. As I often remind you, "Let it out." Whatever is on your mind, say it. Otherwise the thoughts or words that are within you will stay within you. If you can express them and not hurt anyone, they should be voiced.

The level of communication we have is incredible. Is it because I love you so much, or is it because you are a good listener? You smile when I'm mad and say things to you that I shouldn't. You understand me completely and maybe love me a little bit, or perhaps you love me too much, and thus ignore all my faults. Is love blind?

My love for you is so strong and deep that I find it difficult to believe that I, or anyone else, could love another human being so much. As I always say to you, wherever I am, whatever I'm doing, or whoever I'm with, if you ever need me, I am there for you, my love.

I love loving you. You are my own special miracle. The time and days we share are my blessings. The memories we make are my treasures. Every time I see you, you take my breath away and make my heart skip a few beats. The laughter, the silly jokes, and the gentle moments we share are exquisite and make me smile when I am blue. The togetherness we have is my "dream come true," and the understanding we feel for each other is something I have never had with anyone.

If anyone ever asked me what part of my life you are, I would have to look at them, smile, and unhesitatingly say, "the best part." The happiness you give is something I will never be able to get enough of. I love having you in my private world and having you to love. I will never stop loving you in this lifetime, and if there are other lives to follow then I will love in each of those lives too.

One of the best presents I can give you is the poem by Algernon C. Swinburne which reminds me of you

> Ask nothing more of me, sweet
> All I can give you I give
> Heart of my heart, were it more,
> More would be laid at your feet.
> Love that should help you to live,
> Song that should spur you to soar

I do love you,

Anar

7

We're miles apart, day after day, and I miss you so much that sometimes I feel like I'll never see you again. Even after I hear your voice on the phone, it doesn't stop the aching. Maybe while you were here, I took our togetherness for granted. Maybe I didn't always hear the laughter or taste the tears, but I just want you to know that life was much better when you were here. And no matter where you go or what you do, I miss you, and I'll always be here waiting for you.

I remember a time when I felt so alone; the night seemed to never end. Black rain fell endlessly. I was certain that the sun would never shine again. I thought my destiny was to walk life alone. But then you entered my universe, making all of my internal longings vanish like whispers in the night.

And now when you will be with me, I'll never regret the rain or the nights I felt alone. I'll never regret the many tears I shed, the things people said, the many lies, because all these things happened to bring me to you. Every road I had to take, and each time my heart would only lead me closer to you.

My dear heart, all day long I look forward to the time we'll spend together in the evening, next to a fireplace, sipping wine and cuddling. I want to share each and every sunset with you. In fact, I want us to watch the sunset tonight from our balcony. I can imagine it already. When the sun sinks low and the darkness spills across the land like an eclipse, you'll hold my hand and your touch will make me feel the warmth and light that only your touch can generate. The colorful horizon is sure to be magnificent, but it's beauty will pale compared to you, my love.

8

If friendship means harmony, then we have a perfect friendship, because we're so in tune with each other. That's why I'll often call you just when you're thinking of me, or you'll happen to stop by when I need to share something important with you. I'm glad I share that special closeness with you for it makes my life feel richer and complete.

In my heart
In my soul
And in my body
You make me complete

Without you I'm nobody
Why do we have to talk about leaving each other
After all we have gone through
I thought the worst was behind us

I am only this person, my love, because of you
Not because of who I am...you make me whatver you want
I feel beautiful because of you
I feel smart or intelligent because of you

I am you as you are one with me
Else we are nothing
Just two people on this earth
Love you more than you know and always will

Now it is up to you
You can be part of it or leave it
All I have is love for you
Enjoy it, it is rare.

9

The young lovers paid no attention to anything or anyone around them. They were engrossed in each other as they window shopped on State Street and walked along the beach. This was a rare time for them to really get to know each other, and they could feel their relationship blossoming.

One day at lunch time, as Akash and Anar strolled along the beach past the palm trees, surfers, sunbathers, and swimmers, a pleasant warm feeling encompassed both of them. The lovers walked with arms around each other's waists, and Anar had her head tilted on one side as she always did. Every now and then Anar would rest her head on Akash's shoulder, and they would stop and kiss gently as the warm sea breeze touched their happy smiling and glowing faces. They were so much in love that they had no worries in the world. After they walked past the pier, the beach resorts, and hotels, they reached the park where the beach curved and extended into the ocean. Akash found a clean, green spot with no one in sight. They lay next to each other on the grass and touched each other while whispering loving words. Chatting as usual, and losing track of time, before they knew it the gorgeous Californian sunset was visible with all its picturesque glory and beauty. As he looked into the depth of her inviting hazel eyes, all Akash could see were reflections of love that he had grown accustomed to over the past few months. They smiled at each other and hugged without a thought of time. He whispered to Anar...

When we are together, I forget completely who we are. The happiness I feel transports me to another world. When I am with you, it's as though I were an eagle soaring freely in the clear blue sky without a care in the world. You are so special to me, Anar, and you make me feel so wonderful that nothing else and no one else matters when we are together. It seems that we are surrounded by everything that is beautiful and serene in the world. As we travel through life, we see thousands of people and rub shoulders with so many in our daily lives. We get to meet hundreds, and we get to really know a few that we hug. Out of these few, there are some special relationships or bonds. I feel that we have that special friendship. There is a magic about what we have. Almost by instinct, as though we were destined to know each other, you seem to know me and I you. This is the nicest feeling I've ever had. When we're apart, I miss hearing your voice. I yearn for your touch. I long for your scent. And when I am with you, looking at your face, I know that I love you. I never thought I could miss anyone as I miss you. I've always thought of myself as totally independent and self-reliance. I feel I have discovered a part of myself that I didn't know had been missing. I am a different person now than I was before I met you. I feel complete. I feel satisfied in a new way. I am most alive when I am with you. When we're apart, I miss your sensuous lips, your warm comforting hug, your voice on the phone, your giggles and your laughter.

Anar giggled the giggle he loved, and then she kissed him. She didn't mean to kiss him as passionately as she did, but her emotion overpowered her. Here was a man who gave expression to her most private thoughts, and here was a man who described the essence of what she'd been feeling. She'd never fallen in love until she met Akash. He made her feel special as though she was the only person in existence on the planet. He spoiled her in every way possible, fussed over her, cared over her, and made her laugh with his unique and often strange sense of humor. They'd known each other for only four months, but their friendship seemed to go back in space and time. They knew what they felt, the greatest lovers in history had experienced throughout the centuries.

Their stay in California was unforgettable for both of them. They had left England as friends and they would be returning as a couple, with their relationship cemented in every way, physically, mentally, intellectually, and spiritually. The memories they would take with them would forever give then an unforgettable bond.

10

Akash rested in an armchair on the private beach on the small Greek island where they were on holiday and listened to the ocean waves beat against the rocks. It was one of the warmest days of the year, and the hot Mediterranean sun was beating down on him and gradually penetrating the strong sun block he had applied.

The beauty of their surroundings made it seem as if all the swimmers, sunbathers, picnickers, and joggers were in a heavenly paradise without a care in the world. What a place to relax and bask in the triumph of his recent accomplishments.

As the cool breeze flowed in from the ocean towards the mainland and brushed his body, Akash started dozing off, every now and then being woken by delighted screams coming from the girls who were playing volleyball on the beach. As he slipped into a light sleep, his mind drifted into the grasp of dream, and he heard a distant female voice singing.

"You are for me and I for you, my love...we were made for each other...it is written in the wind... it is written on the waves...the winds echo our names as they blow through the canyons, the valleys and the mountains...you are for me and I for you."

He looked for the singer, but there was no one around. The voice kept getting closer and closer. He was tossing and turning, trying to find the singer with the beautiful husky voice, but he couldn't see anyone. He tried to shout; he wanted to ask everyone around him if they knew where she was.

The dream ended abruptly as he felt someone caress his face gently and kiss him lightly on the lips. He opened his eyes and looked into a pair of shining hazel eyes. Anar was looking down at him. They both smiled, he folded her into his arms, and in that embrace time stood still. Did they hold each other only for a few minutes, or was it an eternity?

11

My love Noor,

Your name means light
You are the light in my life
When tomorrow starts without me
And I'm not there for you
If the sun should rise and find your
eyes all filled with tears for me
I wish so much you wouldn't cry
Never again will I bring a red rose for
my love
Think of us and the memories
While thinking of the many things
We didn't get to say

I know how much you love me
As much as I love you
And each time that you think of me
I know you'll miss me too
It is such a nice feeling to be in love
From zillions of sand particles
Two come together and embrace each
other

with love and passion to form a bond
that transforms into an eternal storm

You are my special miracle, I love lov-
ing you
Your love for me has been my treasure
The joy of your love thrills me
This true love of mine will
never die even when I am gone
My Love for you that should help you
soar
Hold me close to your heart always
Let our heartbeats talk to each other
I love you from dawn to sunset

All night long, I thought about you
I'm even dreaming of you when I am
awake.
No matter where I go, no matter how
near or far
I can't stop hearing the beat of your
heart
Every breath I take is in rhythm with
me calling your name

I can picture us together, being
together
I can feel the heat and power of our
passion
As I take you into my arms, the world
fades around us
and I am lost to the taste of your
sweet lips
My fever for you is burning me up
inside
I am so happy because of all the times
we spent together

and all the happiness we did share
I am so happy because we found each
other
I want to be with you during the
nights and snuggle in bed
In the morning, to wake up in each
other's arms

With you, I am living life to the fullest
Because of your love, my
spirit has been rejuvenated
I can see all the hugs, smiles, and
kisses we share
I want to celebrate because we are
together
I want to celebrate tomorrow
because
I look forward to the days ahead with
you
Everyday, I close my eyes and dream
about us together

It feels so right as I kiss you, caress
you, hold you
As you gaze into my eyes and tell me,
how much you love me
My knees grow weak and my heart
skips a beat Your words touch something deep inside of me
I will hold you closer still, heart and
soul whole at last
You're the only one who touches me
The only one who moves me
You're my fondest wish of what the
future could be
I ache for your touch. I crave for your
loving embrace

I love everything about you, your
voice, your feelings and
beauty

I want to be with you all the time
As I look at the moon that is the only
thing we have in common right now
You can look at the same moon that I
am looking at
But when tomorrow starts without
me

Please try to understand
That an angel came and called my
name
And took me by the hand
And said my place was ready, In
heaven far above
And that I'd have to leave behind
All those I dearly love
My eyes are in tears even now
For all my life, I'd always thought
I didn't want to die
I had so much to live for
So much yet to do

It seemed almost impossible
That I might leave you and this earth
I think of all the yesterdays and a
lifetime of memories
The good ones and the bad
You will feel it when I die
I know I will die alone

But I want you to hold my hand when
I die
So I feel your love

I do love you for all this,
my love Noor.

12

Just being with you,
dreaming with you,
talking with you,
laughing with you,
just sharing with you
makes all the difference in my days.

Trusting in you,
believing in you,
confiding in you,
finding joy in you,
caring for you
makes all the difference in my world.

Wanting you,
needing you,
having you,
holding you,
loving you
makes all the difference in my life.

I believe that love can last a lifetime,
and I want to spend that lifetime loving you.

13

You're always with me, even when we're apart and I am feeling all alone,

I close my eyes and think of all the happiness we've known.

I think of how your loving smile is such a precious sight,

and how your arms around me feel so comforting and right.

I think of how I'm free to be myself when I'm with you,

and how you make so much in life seem wonderful and new.

And somehow I feel better then because I clearly see.

Since I hold you close within my heart, you're always here with me.

I love you so much.

14

Love is wanting to be with somebody all the time.
Love is thinking of someone all the time.
Love is thinking of someone when you go to bed.
Love is dreaming of someone.

Love is thinking of someone when you get up in the morning.
Love is thinking the one you love can do nothing wrong.
Love is overlooking the loved one's faults.
Love is physical attraction for someone.

Love is wanting to touch someone all the time all over.
Love is wanting to kiss someone all the time.
Love is wanting to care of someone.
Love is wanting to cook for someone.

Love is wanting to sharing a bath with someone.
Love is wanting to send Valentine cards and writing love notes.
Love is sharing passionate kisses in the morning.
Love is making whoopee every night.

15

When I look at you, your smiling eyes draw me closer to you.
I hold you, look deep into those inviting brown eyes, and lean forward.

The meeting of our lips takes me to another world.
I love life because it gave me you.
I love you because you are my life.

Every time I look at you, I fall in love all over again.
When I first saw you, you took my breath away.
When you first talked to me, I couldn't think.

When you touched me, I got shivers all through my body.
And when we first kissed, I floated away in my dreams.

When you love someone, it's something. When someone loves you, it's another thing. When you love the person who loves you back, it's special.

Don't fall in love with someone you can live with, fall in love with someone you can't live without.

I wish dreams were like wishes and wishes came true, because in my dreams I'm always with you and this dream has come true.

16

Without love we are nothing!`

God created human beings in the form of flesh and implanted a spirit within them that is free, loving, and lovable. There aren't enough prayers to replace a living being on earth. God entrusts us to be kind and loving to our fellow beings.

We are here to help each other, to care for one another, to understand, to forgive, and to serve one another. We are here to have love for every person born on earth. Their earthly form might be black, white, brown, yellow, handsome or ugly, thin or fat, wealthy or poor, intelligent or ignorant, male or female. Each spirit has the capacity to be filled with love and eternal energy.

At the beginning of life, each of us possesses some degree of light and truth that can be more fully developed. As to how it develops during one's life span, it is up to the individual being. We cannot measure these things. Anything we can do to show love is worth it. It may be a smile, a word of encouragement, or a small act of sacrifice. We grow by these actions.

Not all people are lovable. When we find someone difficult for us to love, it is often because they remind us of something within ourselves that we dislike. We must love our enemies and let go of hate, anger, envy and bitterness. I believe god would be extremely pleased with the spirit when a person dies and the spirit move on, if that person had loved all and refrained from hating any of the people encountered during that person's time on earth. We should encourage our children to grow up to love their fellow beings and hurt no one deliberately.

The only certain thing about life is it's uncertainty, and the only certain thing about death is it's certainty. We all have to go sometime, sooner or later. We all know that, but acceptance of this fact is something else. All we can do is live the memories, my love, that is all that one leaves on this earth. And the sad thing is, over time even they diminish and we just have faint remembrances.

I love you and wish I was there to hold and hug and console you.

It hurts so much not to be near you, I can't reach out to you.

17

A perfect morning is when you wake me up with a kiss.
The second best is when you wake me up with a hug.
I will settle for the one where you wake me up with a phone call.

In my world there is only you.
In my life only your love counts.
In my soul your soul lives.
In my mind I only think of you.

My body wants to feel yours.
I do love you with all.
I live because of you.
I do love you very much and will always.

You have been the light in my life and the spark that ignites the moments of sheer happiness that I will treasure forever. When you cry, my body goes all numb and I feel your tears slide down my cheeks. When you are happy, the smile on my lips is from your heart.

18

Sitting in his chair one would think my friend Bobby is a wise old man. Actually he is right. Bobby is old but not the kind of old in which you cannot do anything but sleep all day. He is quiet active. He plays tennis and golf and he taught me how to play these two sports. The thing that I like best about him is his gift giving.

The gifts he gives me make me feel like a pampered kitten that is being picked up, petted and loved. He takes me out of my misery and cares for me with these gifts by showing love and affection. He is like a jellyfish who is always busy and moving around. He took time out of his business to get something for a baby jellyfish. I cradle these gifts as they cradled me when I got them. They made me feel smushed with happiness. When I curled up with these gifts I knew both gifts and Bobby were caring for me. The gifts that he gives are one of the things that make me love him... and tell me he is not an old man that just sits on a chair.

19

After me
When I die, lay me down gently in the cold
wooden coffin
Shed not a tear for me my love
A red rose on my chest as I lay still would be
nice

When you feel sad or miss me my love
Remember the memories that we created
And the loving moments that we so intimately
shared
The laughter, the jokes, the happy times that
we had
Along with the few moments that were sad

As the inevitable smile comes to your face think-
ing of me
You know with our telepathic connection
My lips too have a smile
Remember me not as someone who has gone
forever
But a friend who loved you more than god
wanted anyone to love another

When you miss me or think of me
Kiss a red rose and lay it gently on my grave
my love
My love for you is eternal and ever lasting
I will wait for you until me meet again

Every word I say is true
This I promise you
I give you my word
I give you my heart

This is a battle we have won
Without you in my life
I just wouldn't be living at all
And with this vow
I'll give you hope
You be our strength

This is the promise
When you take me into your arms
And hold me right where I belong
Till the day my life is through

That is your promise to me
As you leave and go away to faraway lands
Beyond the ocean onto a cold island to the land
of your true love
That was a long while ago and could be again
tomorrow

20

My heart aches, it is heavy with sadness and sore with pain
In my mind I know you will be back
Without a soul and without a heart
You will sell your soul to the devil and give your heart to her
And then justify why you did what you do so well

Break my heart and still convince me
You love only me and no other
So, who is it that you search in these foreign lands
In the dark oceans and land full of fog

Tell me my love why are you still thirsty
What will quench your thirst?
What can I do?
Oh my tears can't even drown your urge to swim away from me
Why, why do you have to leave?

21

My love, I can't live without you and I can't exist without you. Every fraction of a second that I am away from you, it seems like being in a vacuum with no one around me and my mind being totally somewhere else. The inner joy that I feel when I am near you is very simply beyond any words that I can write. I have carved your name in my heart and lungs, every breath that I take and every trickle of blood that flows through my veins has your mark on it. Every second that passes has you in my thoughts somewhere.

You are on my mind when I get up in the morning,

You are on my mind as I spend the day away from you,

You are on my mind when I am close to you,

You are on my mind as I fall sleep and long to dream about you.

My thoughts are constantly filled with an image of you, whether it is talking to you, thinking of you, listening to you talk, or listening to your heart beat. I am trying to come to grips with this dilemma by consoling myself that my wish to be always around you and in your thoughts is a possibility and will come true, no matter what.

I have tried searching for the reasons as to why I have this overpowering urge to just love you endlessly and just wanting to care for you and be with you all the time. I always end up with the same answer. These genuine, unselfish, unconditional. and considerate feelings tied with the ability to respect the other's point of view as well as being able to openly communicate with each other is such an array of strong emotions and feelings that even a slackening in any single aspect is overpowered by the other insurmountable feelings.

I guess true love is hard enough to find and sustain, so if one is chosen to experience it, then why question this rare gift from the gods of love. I just love you so much and will never stop as long as there is air around that I breathe.

Just continue being your affectionate self, and keep on expressing feelings as only you can, my sweet love.

22

It is late September in California, the Santa Anna winds are in full force and blowing at their vicious best. As they whistle down the deep Californian canyons and ravines, all that I can hear is the winds say your name over and over. The sound of your name echoes and rolls off into the distant Santa Monica Mountains and across the Pacific.

I am on my way to the beach and an appointment at Geoffrey's, driving down Malibu Canyon Road with the top down. As the fast German automobile goes around the corners, the tires screech, the car sways to the left, to the right. And as I straighten the wheels around a sharp bend, the black metallic color shines under the reflection of a typical Californian full moon light.

As I speed around the winding road, my thoughts are of you, as always. I am sure that it is all one perpetual thought that starts with you in the morning, goes with me as I doze off at night, and carries on in my dreams till the next morning.

What would life be without you? It is impossible to even try to imagine that possibility. I get up in the morning and the first thing I do is whisper your name. All day long, I think of you and where you are and what you might be doing. The rest of the time, I am planning on when I might see you or talk to you next. I love you. When I am with you, it is pure heaven, as I caress you, sip coffee with you, or just talk about everything and nothing.

Is the communication that we have because I love you so much, or is it because you are such a good listener? You just smile at me when I am mad and saying things to you that I really shouldn't. But, that just highlights the fact that you understand me completely and maybe love me a little too much and ignore all my faults. Love does that.

Each day I love you more today than yesterday, and less than tomorrow. My love for you is so strong and deep that I even find it difficult to believe that I or anyone could love another human being that much.

Like I always say... Wherever I am, whatever I am doing, or whoever I am with, if you ever need me, I am there for you my love, my special love, my dear heart.

23

I think of how your loving smile is such a precious sight,
and how your arms around me feel so comforting and right.

I think of how I'm free to be myself when I'm with you
and how you make so much in life seem wonderful and new.

And somehow I feel better then because I clearly see,
since I hold you close within my heart, you're always with me.

I love you so much, let's always hold hands and sneak kisses
and give hugs for no reason.

Let's always laugh together, cry together, and be there for each other.
Let's always be silly.

Let's never stop talking, or sharing, or understanding each other.
Let's keep wishing on stars, and whispering
secrets and dreaming up wild adventures.

Let's always love each other like we do today.
I love all the tender moments we share, the
quiet times when it's just you and me.

I love knowing you love me and that I love you
too.
Thank you for the special times that belong to
us alone.

24

You are my special miracle
I love loving you
Your love for me is my treasure
Love the way you close your eyes when I kiss you

Memories we make are my treasure
The joy of your love thrills me
You take my breath away when you kiss me
This true love of mine will never die

You are my special miracle
I love loving you
Ask nothing more of me sweet
All I can give you I give

Heart of my heart, were it more
More would be laid at your feet
My Love for you that should help you soar
Hold me you close to your heart

Let our heartbeats talk to each other
I love you from dawn to sunset
You are my special miracle
I love loving you

I love the way you hold and hug me
Long to feel you caress your fingers through my
hair
Long to be near you
You are my treasure

Love you when your lips touch mine
Our love is an ocean of everlasting love
You are my special miracle
A hundred hearts would be too few to carry all
my love for you.

I love loving you
I love loving you

25

My Cielo,

The first time I saw you when you walked up the stairs and into the living room and into my life, I thought you were gorgeous, very classy, walked with purpose and elegance. I had no idea then that we would be together and the way we are now. I liked the way you sat down on the sofa with both your feet on the sofa and a laughter that was infectious and made your face look even more beautiful. I have since been impressed with your overall general knowledge and demeanor. Our first hugs were warm, comforting and the body temperatures did escalate by a few degrees. Your touch and when I caress your body, feels warm and a craving for more of the same.

Your sense of humor and outlook on life complements your physical appearance, which is near perfect. I will miss you for the next three weeks, but I will survive knowing that you will fly back into my arms soon.

Am looking forward to our trips together, wherever destiny takes us.

I like being around you. Look after yourself and
take care.

26

The bright rays of the Florida sun filter through the silk drapes and wake me up. I reach out across the bed to feel her. She turns around to face me with the squint in her eyes and the smile on that sculptured Scandinavian featured face. I reach out, caress her, and our lips touch, starting another promising day. I am thankful for that and for her being the significant part of me and my life.

Life is good. I open the windows and the refreshing and pleasant cool breeze from the Gulf of Mexico blows against the drapes. When I am with her, the only place I want to be is closer. She makes every part of me feel that I am alive.

The fresh aroma of coffee from the patio next to the pool floats across the room and I debate whether to go down and get coffee or just lie in bed with her in my arms. The decision is made when she comes and lies on top of me. We finally go downstairs for lunch.

27

My sweetheart, my love,

I am writing this in the early hours of the morning from the dugout as it is my turn to be on watch. First I want to say, it's so hard to be away from you, not talk to you, not hear or see you.

I miss your beautiful smile. I want to touch your skin again as I touched your heart. You are the most beautiful, wonderful, caring, loving, passionate person...and a true soul mate. I can't live without you. As I wait, it hurts more and I can't wait for my term of duty to be over and come back to your arms.

As I wait and listen and dodge the bullets, I am still happy knowing you love me and I have a love that is magical and the most wonderful feeling in the universe. I will never lose faith in your power. I know we can make our dreams come true. Since we have not talked in a long time, I had a lot of time to think and I only love you more than I ever did before.

We are meant to be one as we always were, our hearts and minds are connected...a union you only find once in a lifetime.

I will never let you go as long as it takes but I still worry every day and it hurts in every way. I want you now. I want to touch you, hold you, and kiss you all night long. I want to feel your heart beat. I hate this, it hurts so much...

At the same time I am filled with joy because I have the most perfect companion in this universe. For that I am happy. You are mine, and that's how it always shall be as I am yours, devoted to you. I bow to your beauty and grace.

I know I will be home soon. I know you will be mine soon. I know I will hold you soon. My faith in you has never wavered. My one true love, I will love you, baby, always yours.

Yours forever

28

Around every corner, after each second, after each decision that one might make, there is an impact that determines the certainty or uncertainty of life. The decision might result in the way the mind and heart thought it might, or the reverse might happen or something totally different occurs.

We can never take anything for granted. The moments that we have lived in the past, or the moment that is present, is the only certainty. The only thing that is predictable and certain is death itself. So the message is, live the moment, learn from the past, and try to plan for the future... keeping in mind the unpredictability and uncertainty that may or may not follow.

I love you so, that is certain. I miss you so, that is predictable. I want you, that is certain.

Love you

29

The couple smiled, squeezing each other's hand. Akash and Anar were on the couch watching the great American singer, Harry Belafonte, and the South African legend, Miriam Makeba, singing on Kenyan television, the classic Swahili song Malaika nakupenda Malaika,

Malaika, nakupenda Malaika angel	I love you my
Malaika, nakupenda Malaika you my angel	Angel, I love
Nami nifanyeje, kijana mwenzio do, my love	What can I
Nashindwa na mali sina we any money	I don't have
Ningekuoa Malaika married you my angel	I would have
Nashindwa na mali sina we any money	I don't have

Ningekuoa Malaika   I would have
married you my angel

Pesa zasumbua roho yangu   Money   is
troubling my heart

Pesa zasumbua roho yangu   Money   is
troubling my heart

Nami nifanyeje, kijana mwenzio   What can I
do, my love

Ningekuoa Malaika I   would have
married you my angel

Nashindwa na mali sina we   I don't have
any money

Kidege hukuwaza kidege Little   bird, I dream
about you little bird

Kidege hukuwaza kidege   Little bird,
I dream about you little bird

Nami nifanyeje, kijana mwenzio   What can I
do, my angel

Nashindwa na mali sina we I   don't have
any money

Ningekuoa Malaika   I would have
married you my angel

Nashindwa na mali sina we   I don't have
any money

Ningekuoa Malaika   I would have
married you my angel

72

30

It is impossible to capture in words the feelings I have for you. They are the strongest feelings that I have ever had about anything. Yet when I try to tell you them or try to write them to you, the words do not even begin to touch the depth of my feelings.

And though I cannot explain the essence of these phenomenal feelings, I can tell you what I feel like when I am with you. When I am with you, it is as if I were a bird flying freely in the clear blue sky.

When I am with you, it is as if I were a flower opening up my petals of life.

When I am with you, it is as if I were the waves of the ocean crashing strongly against the shore.

When I am with you, it is as if I were the rainbow after the storm proudly showing my colors. When I am with you, it is as if everything that is beautiful surrounds us.

This is just a very small part of how wonderful I feel when I am with you.

Maybe the word "love" was invented to explain the deep, all encompassing feelings I have for you.

But somehow it is not strong enough. But since, it is the best word there is, let me tell you a thousand times that I love you more than "love."

31

When we met for dinner, I felt this intense energy as I was hugging and kissing you. It felt as if I was sending love and comfort from my heart into yours. I wanted to continue the evening, to go back to your place, just lie together and hold each other, talk about nothing and everything.

I ache for your touch constantly. I want to rest my head on your broad chest, and listen to your heart as I drift off to sleep...then wake up to your beard tickling me and your beautiful brown eyes crinkling in amusement as I stir and grumble.

I love how we wrapped our arms and legs around each other the last time we were in my bed. I adore being tangled up with you. I also love feeling you spooned behind me holding me like a child holding a beloved stuffed toy, telling me everything will be OK, that I'm safe with you.

I love when you call me your baby girl and say sweet, tender things under your breath thinking I can't hear you or will assume you're talking in your sleep.

I love you so much, miss you.

32

Lyrics from the Billie Holiday classic song

"I Am A Fool to Want You"

I am a fool to want you
I am a fool to want you
To want a love that can't be true
A love that is there for others too

I am a fool to hold you
Such a fool to hold you
To seek a kiss not mine alone
To share a kiss the devil has known

Time and time again I said I'd leave you
Time and time again I went away
But then would come the time that when I
needed you
And once again these words I would have to say

Take me back I love you
Pity me I need you
I know it's wrong it must be wrong
But right or wrong I can't live without you
I can't get along living without you

33

The phone rang at 4:00 in the morning. The ring tone just sounded sad and alarming. My brother was crying on the other end, and I knew it was mama, she was gone. I always used to joke that with her everlasting genes, she would outlive me. My brother abruptly put the phone down after giving me the news, and I really didn't grasp the impact till I got up and walked around for a few minutes, just wandering around the condo.

Our mama was gone. I hadn't seen her for a few years, and now I was angry at myself for not having gone to London to visit her. The guilt at not being there when she could have needed my support made me angrier.

From this moment on, I will never be able to pick up the phone and hear her voice again, or feel her hugs or kisses on the forehead. She had been there for me whenever I needed her, but I wasn't there when she left us. She had been the strength, guide and pillar for me and my siblings, but now that common bond was gone. A "mother's love" is irreplaceable. You always know who your mother is. The bond created by creating a life, giving birth, and the sequential nourishment from her body is never forgotten.

This is when we all reminisce and wish that we had done more with the departed soul, spent more time, talked more, loved and cared more, and been there for them. Time is supposed to be a healer, there is no healing. Over time, the person becomes a distant memory and whenever something triggers an image of the person, the sadness comes back. But we get solace by reliving the pleasant memories that are there for all of us.

I miss her.

34

Those we have truly loved never leave us.

They live on forever somewhere deep within the heart.

Sometimes when I'm alone and lost in thought, all the world seems so far away. You come to me as if in a dream, gently taking my hand and filling my soul with the warmth of your presence.

And I smile knowing that though we cannot be together for now, we are always close in thought. I miss you so much.

35

Oh, how I've longed to express my feelings to you. Shadowed by the sunset's dying light, I lift a lover's pen to spill my love with crimson ink, but the words to express the depth and breadth of my love are not in sight. I'm assaulted by pangs of the heart and soul, pining feelings for you. I want only to push back those embattle-ments that shelter the words and tell you how much I long to be with you.

With midnight upon me, I try to reach into my soul, but still nothing comes from my weary pen to express how much I care about you. I could gaze longingly into your green eyes. I could dance with you on clouds of silvery white. But still the words rush not to my pen, not a romantic word in sight.

Your love is so wonderful and rare; it's bold, with a mischievous grin. It's as humble as a lady's maid, and as courageous as a knight. If only I could find the words to make your day bright. The power of your gentle kiss can drop me to my knees. We're a portrait of love's perfection for all feasting eyes to see. Still I'm unable to express my love for you, but I'll wait with anguished heart, in hopes that I've given you a clue. Please let me know if you might just love me too?

36

My dearest heart,

I'm sorry I am not there when you awake. The sun will rise dimmer for lack of the added radiance of your beauty. My love for you grows with every sunrise, and the limit of that feeling is the last sunset of my life on this earth...and, hopefully, that will synchronize with your last moment.

I will see you soon, my love, though never soon enough.

Your soul,

Raj

37

You are flying out tonight to the distant and rugged mountains in Afghanistan. I know that you are there to defend our country but you'll take a piece of my heart and a stream full of tears with you. Each day I'll look at the screen saver on my laptop with our photograph and think of my loss. I will not wipe the tears so that I can sustain your memory.

Every night that you're overseas and away from me, when I lie down on the bed and doze off I will think of you so that I can dream of you and us. I will see your smiling face and feel your touch. When I awake, I'll reach for you on the other side of the bed and when I feel a cold sheet, I will get a sharp heartache and feel sadness. Only the everlasting memories of our time together, and the knowledge that you love me as much as I do you, will sustain me through these lonely days and nights. I vow that when you return, we'll never be away from each other's arms and we'll make up for the time and love that we will have missed.

Come back soon and safe.

38

I miss you so much Meri Jaan, the sadness in my heart is unbearable.

We have been apart for so long, seems forever.

I know our hearts have been together, but I want to see you.

I want to feel you and your lips.

The feeling I have now is that I am counting days, as the twilight of my life is before me and staring me in the face.

This is not fair as our lives are coming to an end, and we never had a chance to enjoy each other and be with each other.

I wish I knew that in the next life time we would be together, and that would console me as I leave this life longing for you.

39

All My Loving lyrics
Songwriters: Paul McCartney
and John Lennon

Close your eyes and I'll kiss you
Tomorrow I'll miss you
Remember I'll always be true
And then while I'm away
I'll write home every day
And I'll send all my loving to you
I'll pretend that I'm kissing
The lips I am missing
And hope that my dreams will come true
And then while I'm away
I'll write home every day
And I'll send all my loving to you
All my loving, I will send to you
All my loving, darling I'll be true
Close your eyes and I'll kiss you
Tomorrow I'll miss you
Remember I'll always be true
And then while I'm away
I'll write home every day
And I'll send all my loving to you

All my loving, I will send to you
All my loving, darling I'll be true
All my loving, all my loving
Ooh, all my loving, I will send to you

40

Many people have touched my life, yet you have touched my heart and spirit in the beautiful way that only you can.

Your touch excites me, longing me to want more.

Your smile wants me to keep looking at you and wanting more.

I look in your eyes and I want to keep looking into them and see the love forever.

As we hug, I want to keep holding on and want more.

As our lips touch the excitement lingers and wants me to want more.

When we are together, I just want that moment to freeze and last forever.

41

I've been waiting for a long time to see the sun shine; to take a stroll

barefoot on the white sand at the breathtaking Marco Island Beach. I want

to see the beauty of your face as the cool gulf breeze brushes it and your

blond hair spray across your cheeks.

I've been waiting to feel your touch on my arm and the warmth of your

hands as we caress each other.

I am waiting for our love to blossom; waiting for a lifetime that would

never end.

Now, I have all of this and so much more to come, my dream came true,

the day I met you, my heart.

42

I remember when we first met you always said,

"You know we are going to break up" and I used to say,

"I don't think so but let's wait and see and just enjoy the moments".

Now, that we have broken up, I am trying not to wipe the tears, I want

these to stay there as a reminder of our love.

When I walked away from you at the airport, I didn't want to turn back

and see your face for the last time as I knew I couldn't handle that.

There is sadness and I ache but deep down in my heart I know this is

best for both of us. We have just drifted apart and moved on in our separate ways.

I will always miss you and cherish our moments together that ranged from

the silliest to the most wonderful that any two individuals in love could

ever dream of.

I will miss that.

My sweetest memory is of me holding your face in my hands, looking into

your eyes and gently touching our lips and then looking at each other as

we smiled.

When we first met, the both of us couldn't wait to see each other,

touch each other and be with each other. We developed a relationship

built on so many things. A sense of humor that kept us amused for hours.

we did so many things together, travelled, swam, golfed, danced and

dined.

I will miss that.

Now, we have to look ahead, meet our destiny and in times that will be

lonely, relive the memories that are countless. After a while, this will seem

like a distant dream that was pleasant and extraordinary.

I will miss you.

43

Something you should know about Just
The Way You Are:Artist: Billy Joel

Don't go changing, to try and please me

You never let me down before Don't imagine
you're too familiar

And I don't see you anymore

I wouldn't leave you in times of trouble

We never could have come this far

I took the good times, I'll take the bad times

I'll take you just the way you are

Don't go trying some new fashion

Don't change the color of your hair

You always have my unspoken passion

Although I might not seem to care

I don't want clever conversation

I never want to work that hard

I just want someone that I can talk to.

44

Every night when I close my eyes, I think of you

Every morning when I open my eyes, you're the first thing on my mind

I hope that someday you'll be more than just a dream, more than just a

distant image

I'm in love with you and of that I'm sure

I want to hold you,

I want to make love to you

I want to care for you and adore you

If you'll be mine, you'll make my life complete

If you turn me away, I'll be sad and devastated

But either way, you'll always be the love that embraced my

heart and made me feel warm all over

45

I love you. Just writing that makes me smile. I love you because of your kindness, your sweetness, your tenderness and thoughtfulness. I love you because you are my best friend. You smile at my silly jokes and enjoy my youthful spirit.

I love you because I have a longing to be close to you and you long to be close to me. I love snuggling with you in front of a fire and cuddling you as we watch television. I just love being near you. I love holding your hand on a walk in the evenings and holding your hands across the table at a restaurant at night.

I love you because you listen to me as I share the daily triumphs or disappointments. I love you because in moments of friction between us, you hear me out. Even when we disagree you listen with a longing to understand me.

I love you because you respect me, you appreciate me. You honor me for what I am rather than trying to change me into someone I am not. You suffer my imperfections and my shortcomings without complaining.

You enjoy my attentiveness and me romancing you.

I love you.

Printed in Great Britain
by Amazon

25069726R00068